# *Notions*

*Creative Works in Words and Art*
*David Lipscomb High School*
*2010*

*Notions:*
*Creative Works in Words and Art, David Lipscomb High School, 2010*
Copyright © 2010 by David Lipscomb High School
3901 Granny White Pike
Nashville, TN 37204

Published by the Gospel Advocate Company
1006 Elm Hill Pike
Nashville, TN 37210
www.gospeladvocate.com

Cover Photograph by Stephen Eastop
Cover Design by Carrie Abood and Travis Merriman

ISBN-10: 0-89225-573-0
ISBN-13: 978-0-89225-573-3

# About *Notions*

Notions can be defined as beliefs, opinions, fanciful impulses, and flashes of brilliance on everyday life. The notions compiled in our first literary publication certainly fit the above descriptions. In years to come, my wish for *Notions* is two-fold: first, to be an outlet for those who have something to say in words and art; second, to also be an inspiration to those of us (present company included) who may find it difficult to express their notions to the world. *Notions* was not created for the administration, the English department, or myself: *Notions* is here because I am reminded daily that you have more to say than can fit between our school's walls and that you deserve an oulet for your notions.

# Special Thanks

To Kerry Anderson, Travis Merriman, and Menda Kincaid at the Gospel Advocate Company. Without you, there would not be a *Notions*.

To Mike Hammond, Mark Pugh, and the DLCS administration. Thank you for giving me the freedom to try something new.

To Dr. Dana Carpenter for her insight into creating a literary journal

To the DLHS English department, for keeping my sanity in check.

Carrie Abood
Editor

# Table of Contents

# Ferris Wheel

**matt gordon**
*photograph*

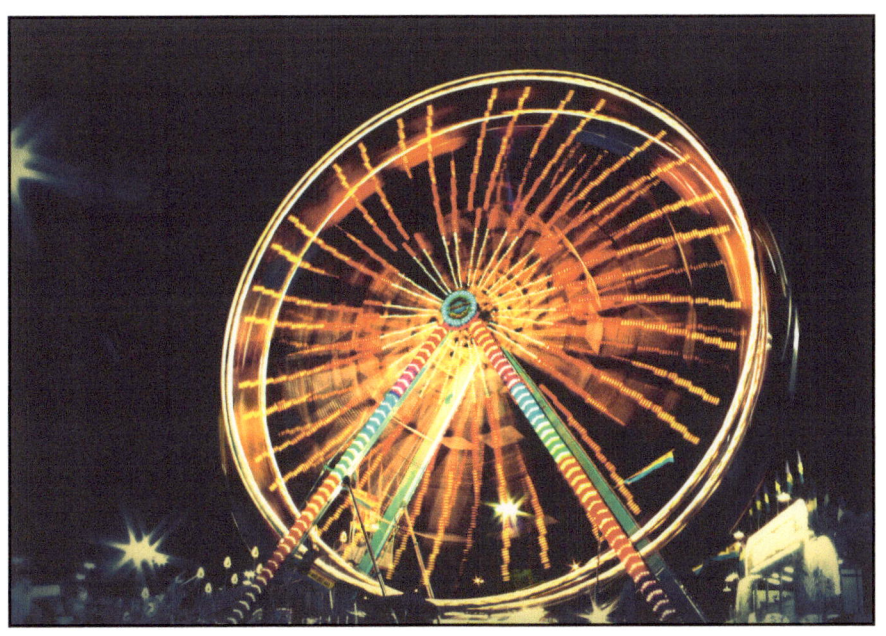

# First Impressions

## dolci sanders
*fiction*

the first impression of the girl was that she was ugly
Maybe even terribly ill
Her eyes never rose to meet the world beyond her feet or meet another's eyes
Her silence was mysterious
The hair on her head way always tangled into knots
Even worse was her oily face
Baggy clothing hid away her small and slender figure
Hand me downs long since worn out
Days passed and ridicule among her classmates spread like wild fire
Her name not even remembered
Could no one see her suffering or cowering in fear
Not a soul to intervene
Day after day she heard the awful whispers about her
The words made her cringe where she sat
The day came when a new student arrived in the classroom
The whispers turned towards the boy
His perfect hair and the pale blue eyes made many girls giggle
For what he 'had' was what she 'lacked'
His voice stood out from all the rest encouraging the girl
With a smile he asked her name
The shock of his inquiry was puzzling to her still
Her head was down, her voice was small
A kind hand lifted up her chin to meet her amber eyes
Her eyes glittered with full surprise
Becoming friends from that day he learned her own life story
Her appearance changed quite slowly then
She was like a butterfly breaking out of her cocoon
The students saw her new figure

Self confidence had lost her; first impressions before

While changed before was remembered
Never quite forgotten was the first impression she made
Things are not always as they seem

The first impression of the man was that he was trash
He was always near the road side
With a sign in his hands he begged for the care of others
A misterable life he lead
His warm eyes told a story for those daring to meet them
One of horror and much great pain
Un-caring honks from cars passing by relayed the world's view
He seemed not to matter to any
Cold or helpless there was no one to come save him here, now
Not one friendly face in the crowd
What had he done to have gone so wrong as to end up here
Not always had he lived like this
As the days passed his soul became lifeless at peace with death
Heaven would be an improvement
Hopeless he endured the stares the laughter the ridicule
Others were 'mightier thou'
On the streets coins clinked in the chipped mug he held in his hands
But those people did not care
Walking by it was out of pity not love quarter dime
Hands to face he was full of sorrow
Then came from down the road a sign of God's great love and care
A boy and girl with caring smiles
Stopped to help this broken man with care and acknowledgement
Looking at him not through him
Taking his hand they led him to a place that he might sleep
Finding rest with his God's own sheep
Fulfillment and encouragement refreshed his soul
People now judging him no more
Memories remained with him about his former lifestyle
New ones made but old ones remained
Never quite forgotten was the first

# impressions he made

Things are not always as they seem

The cruel world is based on first impressions more than anything
The question is can the world change
Are first impressions second nature to the human race
Are they excuses for cruelty

# His Silhouette

**katie mcmurray**
*photograph*

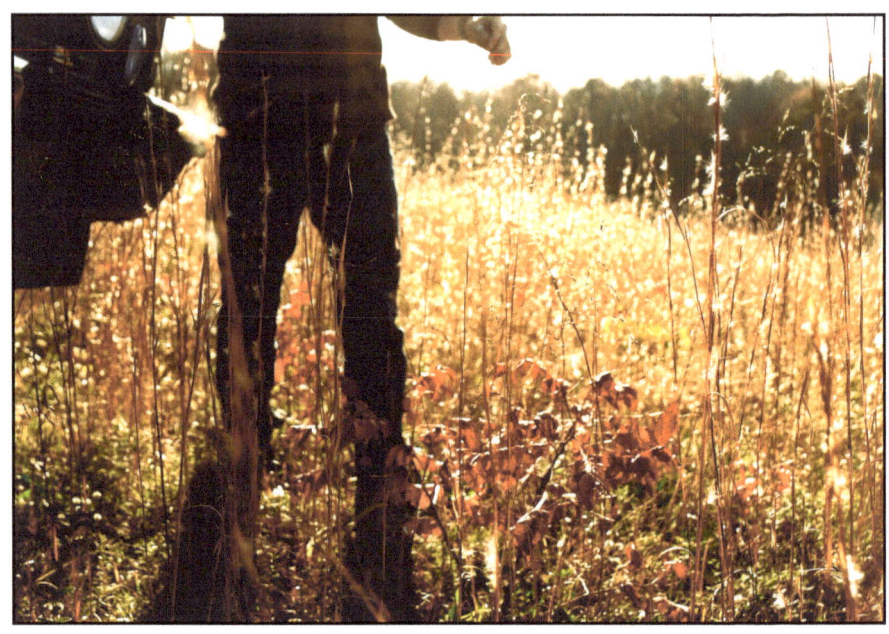

# The Night Crowd

### katie mcmurray
*photograph*

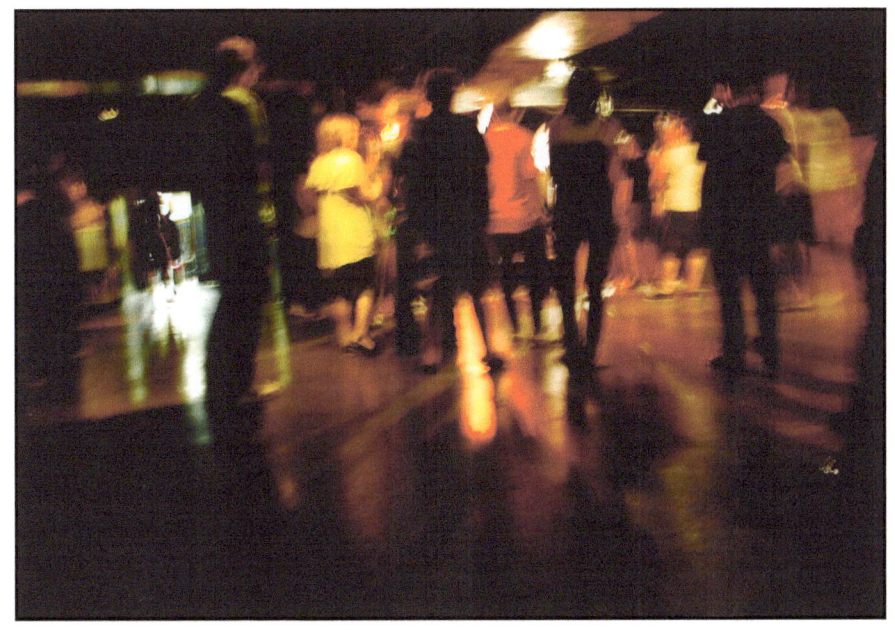

# Mountain of Angels

## kara morris
*creative nonfiction*

Sweat was trickling down Peyton's back as she made her way up the mountain. It was scattered with ragged shacks all the way to its sharp peak. She was so exhausted from traveling the increasing slope while small children half her age ran swiftly past her without skipping a beat. Peyton felt sharp pains shooting up and down each arm. The strain was due to the oversized trash bag she was carrying. It seemed full of hundreds of smooth rocks, but instead it contained only rice and tortillas. From this point the only thing that kept pushing her to continue was her friends that surrounded her, the grace of God, and the fact that this one bag would feed a family of twelve for a month.

Her strength was just about to disappear when the load was suddenly lifted from her. Startled, she looked up to see one of her new friends that she had made when she came to this impoverished country. She thanked him graciously and took the much lighter load that he was carrying. As Peyton and the group closed in on their destination, they could hear an excited murmur of voices mixed with the sound of chickens that surrounded them. They finally arrived at the tiny house on the side of the great mountain and knocked on the scrap of wood that was being used as a makeshift door. The voices coming from the home broke off into a low whisper as a tiny old woman peeked around the door. Seeing a group of Americans, she stepped aside and waved us in. The house could not have been bigger than a closet; however, they still managed to pack the whole group in the home along with the family of twelve.

As Peyton handed the package to the little woman, tears began streaming down her leathery face. The tiny woman then asked to pray over them. It sounded so beautiful. Peyton had no idea what the woman was saying because it was all in Spanish, but she could feel God in every inch of the little one room home. The group then began to sing "Someday" in Spanish. Between the large family and Peyton's group it sounded as if angels were singing the sweet melody.

# The Letter

*shannon connelly*
*comic*

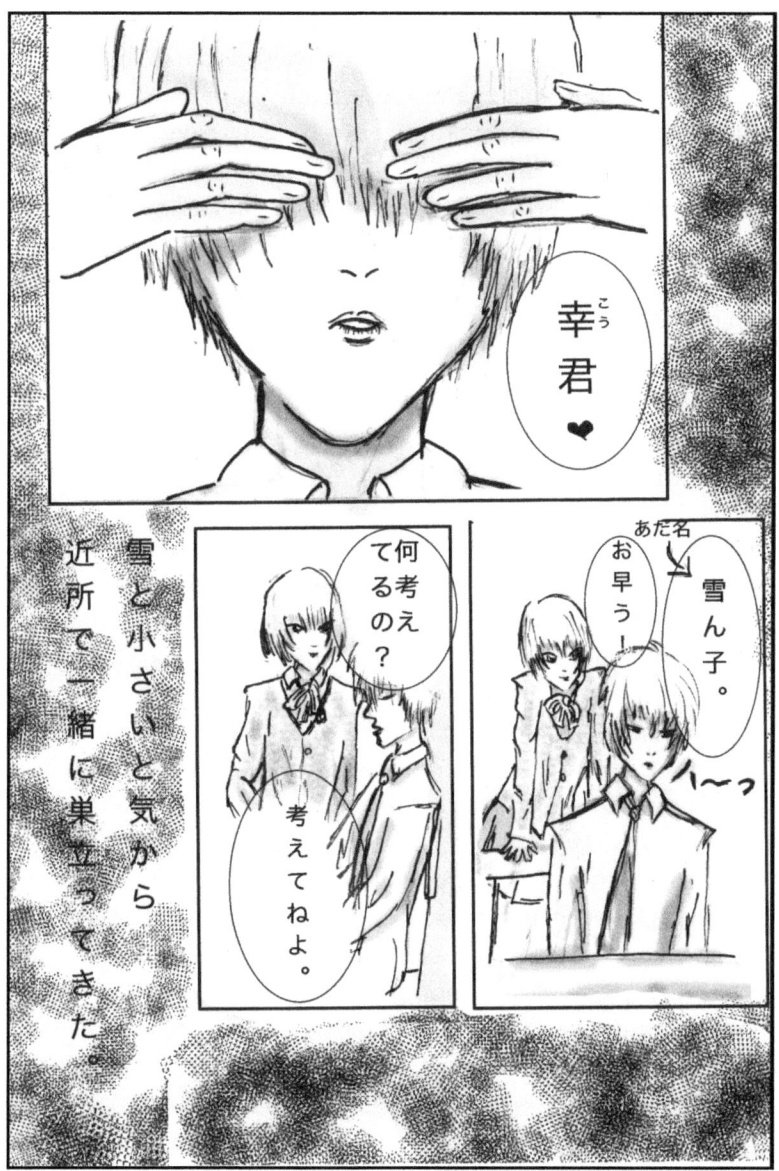

# Bounty Hunter

## cody owen
*fiction*

Rilayen Latronis looked up and saw a man coming out of the cave he had been watching. He was dressed in ragged clothing, but he looked strong and Rilayen recognized him. He was an assassin who tried to enter the Shadow Knife but was turned down. The Order of Purifae caught him and threw him in prison a short while later, but he must have escaped between the time that Rilayen was sent out and now.

Rilayen had a sudden idea that he could earn a little extra cash by bringing in both men. He stood from his hiding place as the escapee walked by and drew his longsword on the man.

"You are under arrest in the name of the Order of Purifae," recited Rilayen, and the man turned to face him. Rilayen hated saying that; he would rather just say what he always said afterwards and have done with it. "Throw down your weapon, or I'll run you through with my own."

"If you did that," replied the escapee, "you'd have no one to take back to those thrice-forsaken Purafix!" The escapee drew his own sword, the one he had just bought, and Rilayen had to force himself not to laugh. It was a pitiful weapon, a cutlass, with small chinks in the blade and a tip that wasn't quite sharp enough to pierce leather. The entire thing, hilt and all, was painted red with rust.

"You've got a head, haven't you?" Rilayen said it with confidence, convincing the escapee that if he did not kill the bounty hunter that the bounty hunter would take his head back to the Order. He wouldn't do it, though. He had no desire to take the man's head with him, and anyway every one of the Purafix would trust him with their life, so he didn't need to bring proof. All he needed to say was that he ran into the escapee assassin and killed him, and he would be paid for that as well.

But the escapee didn't know that so he attacked content to keep his head on his shoulders. He was as much an incompetent at fighting as his cutlass was at being a weapon, and he simply ran forward with the rusty weapon held over his head, shouting like a madman.

He swung it down on Rilayen, but Rilayen swung up his longsword, catching the weapon on his own. The escapee slid his cutlass down the edge of Rilayen's sword, thinking it was a good idea, then suddenly found that it was down between the U-shaped cross guard and the blade of the bounty hunter's sword. Rilayen twisted his arm and wrist, the rust took over, and the top half of the cutlass snapped and broke free. It flew ten feet before hitting the ground on one of the "sharpened" edges, then bounced a few times and lay flat in the dirt.

"The edge didn't even stick in the ground," muttered Rilayen. "I think what you've got there is actually, or was actually, a metal club. Swords are supposed to be sharp."

The escapee turned to flee, but Rilayen threw out a foot, tripping him and throwing him to the ground. "You're pitiful," he said. Then he reached down, grabbed the man by the back of the collar and hauled him to his feet. Rilayen shoved him into a tree face first, pulled out some rope and tied him to it. "Now stay there until I come back to get you," he said before turning into the cave.

He sheathed his longsword and started into the darkness. It was only a few moments later when he saw a light, and suddenly there were lights on both sides of the wall. He looked back and saw that he had unconsciously turned a corner and the entrance was no longer visible and the lights could not be seen from outside. The man's shop was well hidden.

"Ah, another customer!" said a voice from the shadows. As Rilayen got closer, he saw that it was a tall, thin man with dirty, graying hair.

"No, sorry," said Rilayen. "You are under arrest in the name of the Order of Purifae."

"Ah, a Knight are you?"

"No, I'm a bounty hunter. I just happen to be doing some work with the Order. But I can take you to a Purafix Knight, if you would like."

"No, no, no!" The man shook his head vehemently. "What can I give to you that would make you, eh, not find me?" He reached down and drew out his own sword, holding it out as though giving it to Rilayen. "How about my weapon? It is the best of my entire stock."

Rilayen's longsword was already drawn and he flicked his wrist at the man, knocking the sword flying. "Mine's better. There's nothing I want from you. Just come quietly and no one gets hurt."

The man bent over and picked up his sword, fingering the tip. "That's because if I come quietly I don't kill you," said the man. "You should have taken my offer, hunter."

The man came forward, swinging his sword around to one side. Rilayen spun his blade around so it came out of his hand backwards and caught the blow in a clash of steel. He pulled away, spun the sword back around and lashed out, hammering into the flat of the other man's weapon. Rilayen heard the brittle, rust-covered steel crack under the pressure.

The man's eyes widened as he heard it too. He took advantage of Rilayen's "surprise" that was actually more of a "figures." His sword swung around to the right, but suddenly Rilayen wasn't there. He had backed away at the last second, and he slammed his sword into the rusty blade again. This time it shattered, metal shards flying everywhere.

But now, Rilayen's back was to the weapons dealer. The man lashed out with a knife he brought from nowhere; then he gasped. Rilayen had driven his sword under his armpit and through the weapon dealer's chest. Rilayen sighed, then pulled the longsword out and started towards the cave exit as the man fell to his knees.

**Taken from Chapter 1: *The Righteous Bounty Hunter***

# Light and Shadow

**sarah heath**
*photograph*

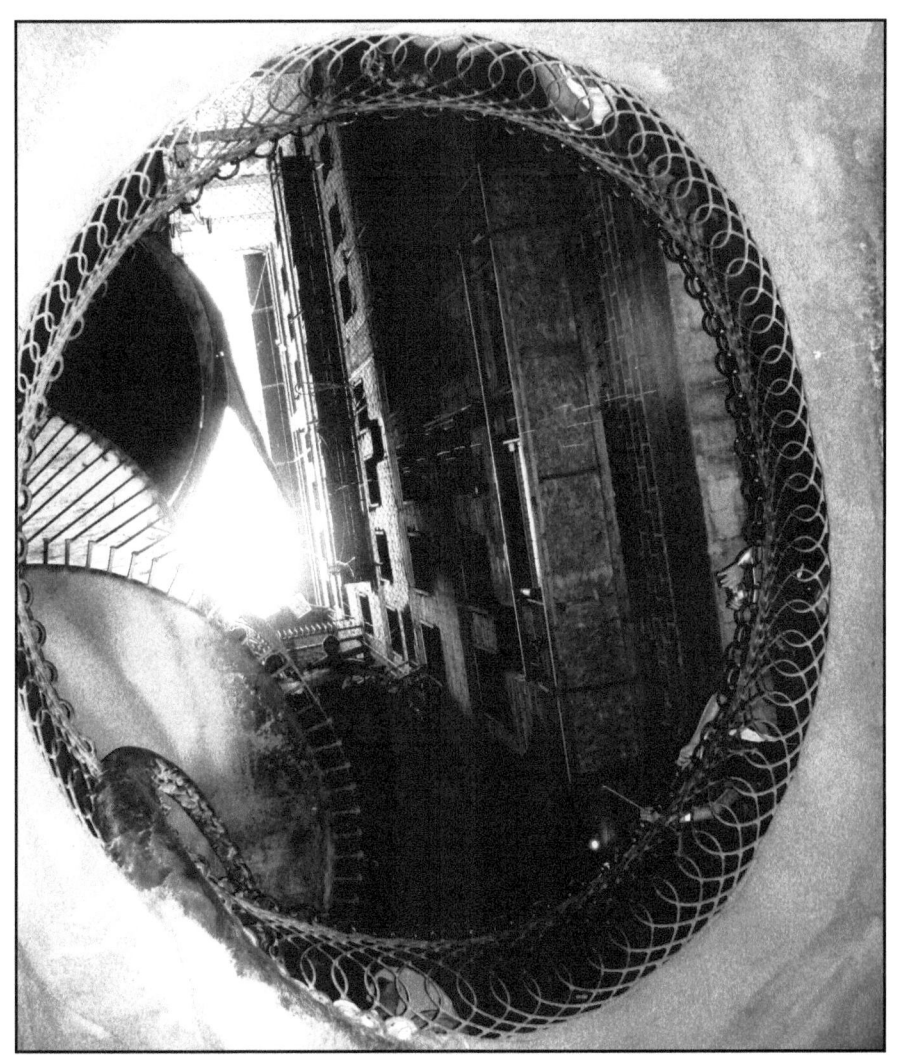

# Owl

**micah bradley**
*acrylic painting*

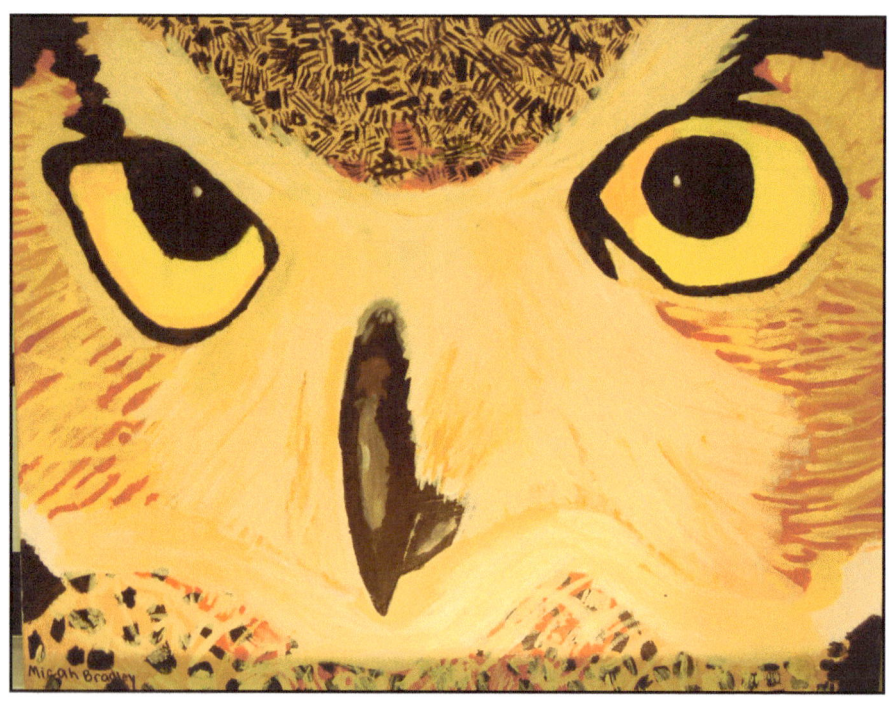

# Classroom Sounds

colleen casner
*poetry*

*psst, psst, psst*
Everyone around me is whispering
about their poems.
The teacher's voice, loud and clear
flies through the fog of whispering
to answer a question.
Clouds form.
The fog of whispering is now a stead rain of chatter.
*patter pat pat patter patter pat*
The piercing noise of the bell
cuts through the rain of chatter
like lightning,
with the thunder of more voices
to answer it.

# Romanian Peasant

**anna little**
*photograph*

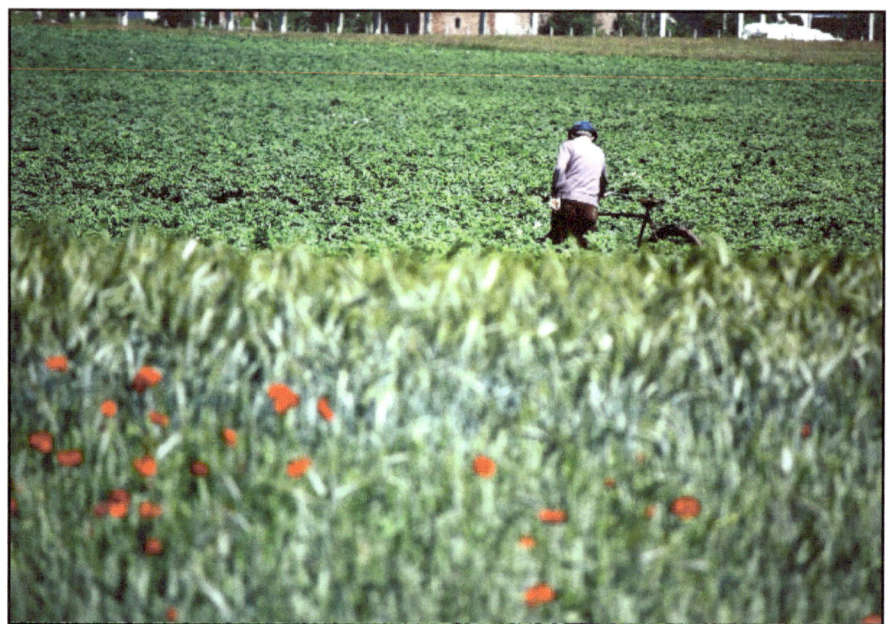

# Nature's Fisheye

**anna little**
*photograph*

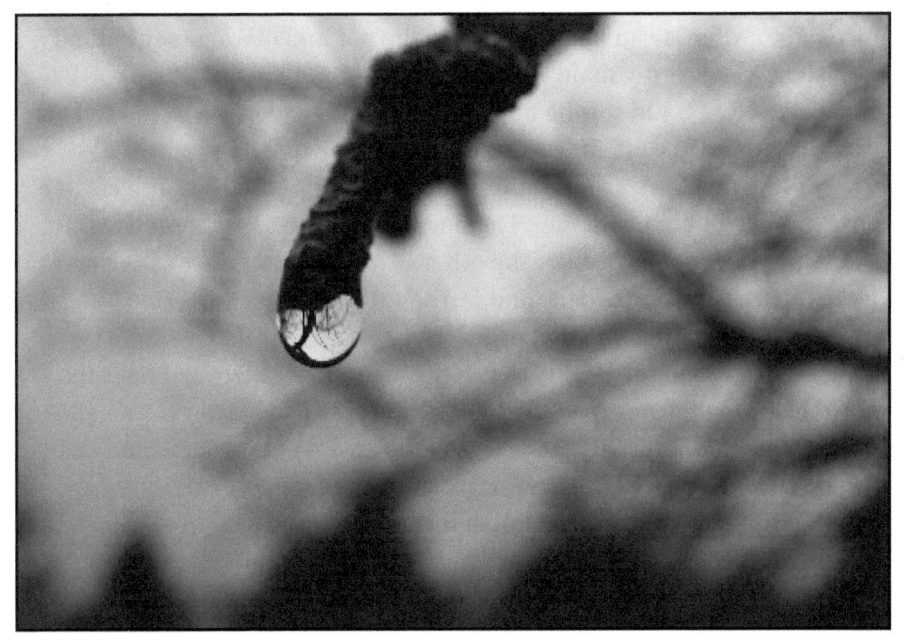

# One Hundred Meters to Go

## miranda klein
*creative nonfiction*

The smell of the newly-cut grass is in the air. Looking down, I see the water still lingering on the tops of the flower petals. I take in a deep breath while a man slogs across the squishy ground, stopping a few feet from the starting line. He raises his arm and moves his fingers to the trigger of the gun, and like a soldier on the frontline of battle, my stomach turns violently.

Bang! A sudden jolt inside me makes my legs sprint forward, so off I go, up the hills and back down, trudging through the tall grass, twisting and turning through the trees, running as if in some kind of funhouse at the fair.

I begin to feel a stream of pain flowing down through my legs like a river. Each muscle, beginning at my toes, begins to cramp. Suddenly, my ears perk up. I hear heavy breathing behind me. What is this? What is happening? While running around yet another curve, slowly I position my head to where I can just slightly see the red and black jersey behind me. There she is – my main competition, from University School of Jackson City. How could this be happening? I had made sure to run in such a way as to hold her off, at least until close to the finish line.

I turned back around, this time with a new mindset. It feels like a fire has been lit beneath me. The burning in my legs is ignored as I forcefully put one foot in front of the other. That is the way it was the rest of the race, back and forth, back and forth, until there we were, one hundred meters before the finish line.

The adrenaline begins to run throughout my body as I hear the crowd chanting my name – fifty meters now. As I strive to get the jello-like feeling out of my legs, the voices of the crowd entangle me and send a ringing through my ears. There, right in front of me, is the only thing keeping me from crossing the finish line with the state title.

Then, something extraordinary occurs inside me...a new feeling, a new strength. I want to win! The gap begins to close between this girl and me. Ten meters now, the crowd roars. I am so close, I can feel the sweat dripping from her back and hitting my face. One last surge, quick! The next few seconds are a loud blur. I am on the ground, mind racing, wishing I could see straight. I then awake to the sound of my coach's voice saying, with a grin, "I knew you could."

# Colorful City

**chris safley**
*color sketch*

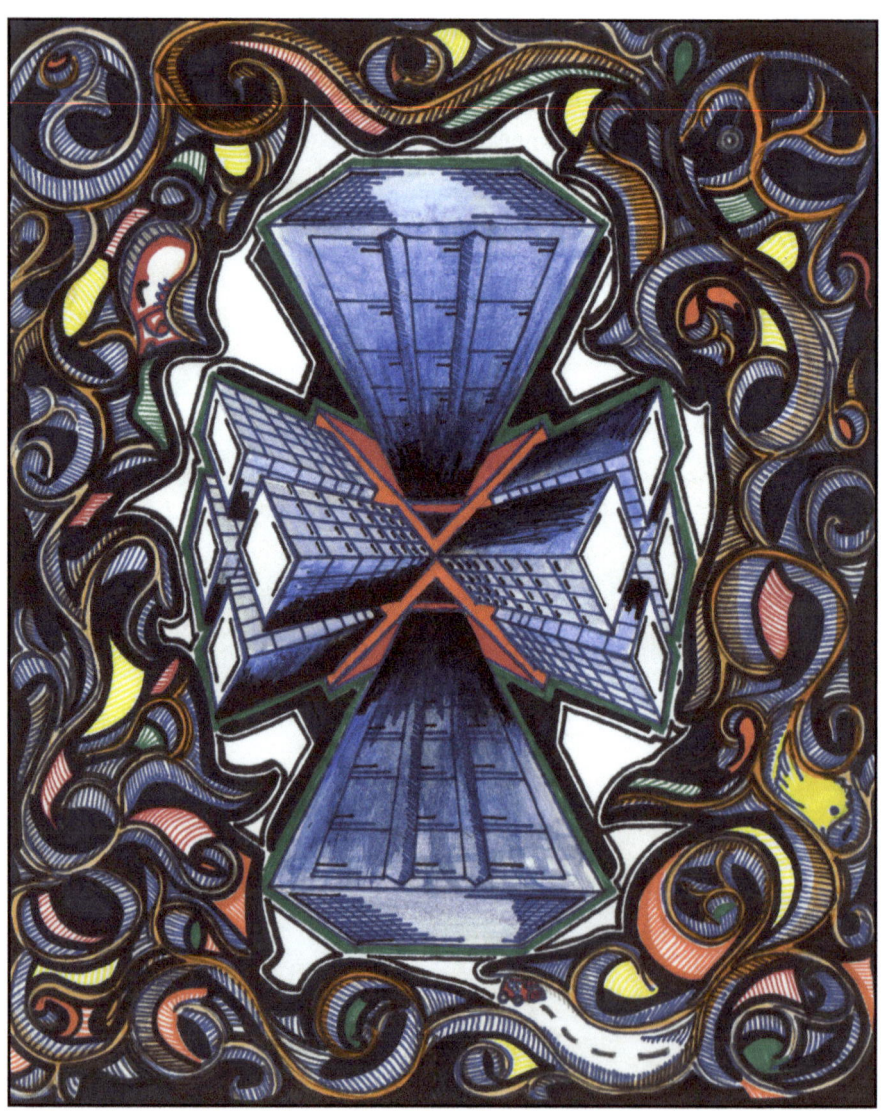

# Faith & Pain

andrew stewart
*poetry*

The tingle you have
when arm is asleep – Numb, but,
know it will be fine.

# Purple Pansies

**dolci sanders**
*photoshop*

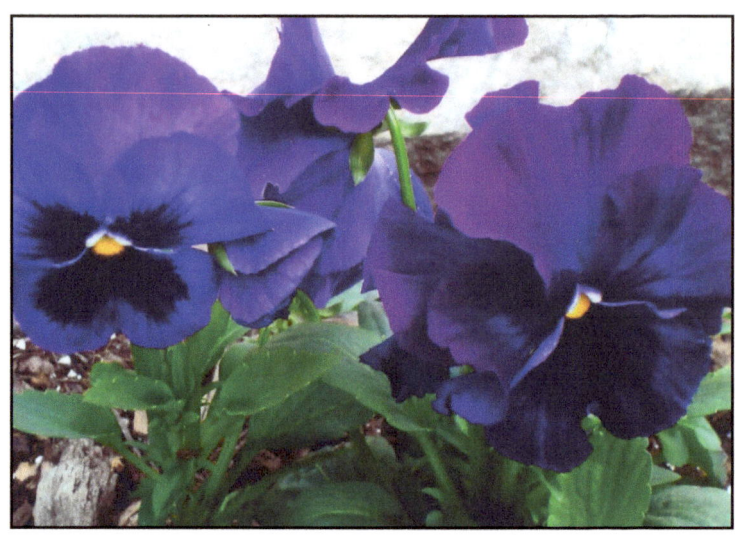

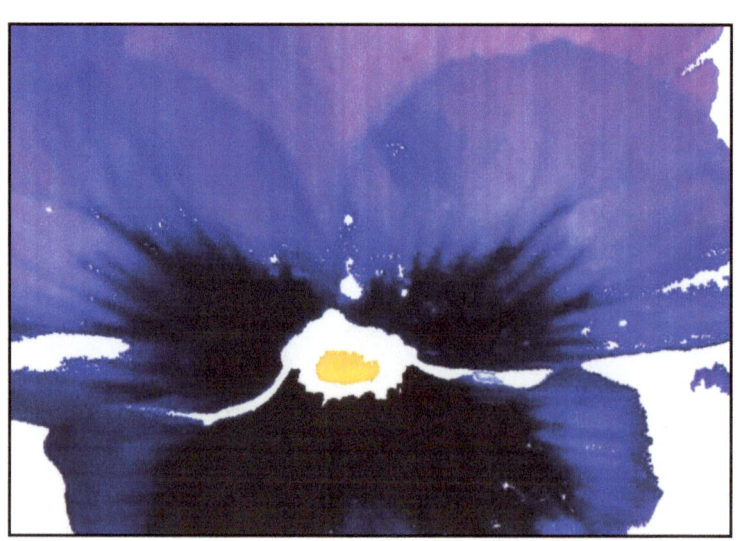

# My Summer Shoes

**graham sears**
*photograph*

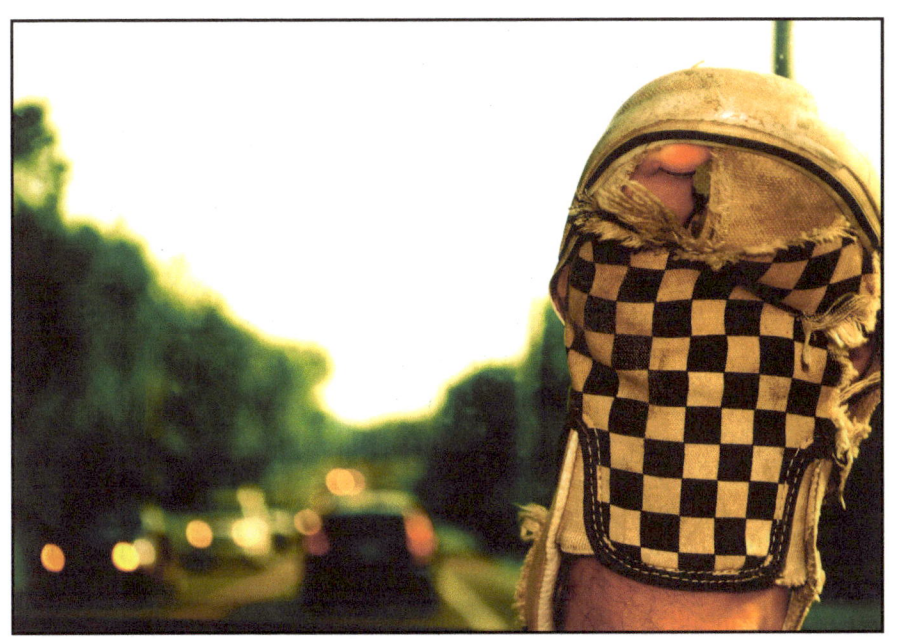

# My Henry

## janie lynn lankford
*fiction*

"Henry! Henry!" I call.

Where is that ridiculous man? I'm walking out to the front porch in search of my beloved. This is strange. He is usually home by now, sitting in the kitchen, waiting for his eight o'clock supper. I hope he hasn't fallen again. Maybe I should go look for him. No. Do not let yourself think the worst. I'm sure he is on his way. Maybe one of the cows needed his extended attention. Yes, that's it. Probably that ugly, brown, mean one I despise so. Oh, no matter! He will be along soon enough, I think as I walk back into the kitchen to make it spotless before he comes. Oh, I love the way his eyes gleam with pride when he sees the kitchen clean, my hair combed neatly, and me waiting there at the door the moment he comes in. Maybe I should cook his favorite for dinner. Smiling, I continue to daydream of my love as I set the table, just the way Henry likes it.

Knock! Knock! Oh, there he is now! He's come to sweep me off my feet again. Maybe he will tell me about his day and all the times he thought of me. Pondering this, I walk to the door. Oh dear me! I must have begun to sweat in my haste to reach perfection for my dear, dear Henry.

"Oh, Rachel! I didn't know you were coming! I'm just waiting on Henry, he'll be home soon, you know. That horrid brown cow kept him waiting. Oh, I never forgave it for ruining my favorite blue dress. Enough of my grumbling! How are you, my lovely Rachel?"

She stared at me in shock and disbelief. I repeated myself, in case she hadn't heard me. She slowly shakes her head, pity in her eyes and disappointment on her face.

"What is the matter? It's not Henry. He'll be home soon. Did you know that, Rachel? My Henry is on his way home…"

She sent me to bed. Bed! I'm older than her, to be exact! I don't see why she can tell me what to do. Oh well, I am quite tired. I'm in no mood for a quarrel, but of course she must have known that. Rachel knows not to pick a fight with me. We both know that I've had the upper hand since we were little children. Oh me, Rachel! Always had the boys after her, and I was always there to pick up the pieces. I know that she'll repay me someday, but that is a long way off. I could just lie down for a minute or two. Just until Henry gets home. Then I must wait for him so I will be the first thing he sees. Oh how I love Henry...

I awake with a start. It feels as if I am stepping out of sand. I blink over and over. For some strange reason my eyes are a bit sore. Also, I feel stiff, as if I had been in the same position for hours upon hours. Floating over the wash basin, I look in the mirror. NO! No! This isn't right! The "sweat" that covered my dress was striking to my eyes. There is brownish-red all down the front of my dress! Blood. I must have been screaming, because Rachel is suddenly by my side. Like a mother caring for a child, she wraps me in her arms and rocks me back and forth in a steady motion. It all comes flooding back. I can hear her quiet "shh" as she tries in vain to stop the hysterics, but beneath that, somewhere behind my eyes, I can still see him laying there.

"Tell me," I say. She begins.

"They came through last week, the army I mean. A regiment met them. Right out front of here. Henry must have seen how close they were to the house from the barn. He feared for you, so he must have come running."

I can see the tears streaming down her pink, flushed face, and that's when I notice my eyes. They are swollen and red, as if I had been crying for a week. Who knows? Maybe I have. I can't remember. She continues in a controlled, hushed voice.

"As soon as the firing was over I came. Oh! I tried to come sooner, but they were so persistent with their bloody battle. Two days later I found you with him. I couldn't imagine how you must have felt, seeing him like that. You, you were..."

I cut her off. "Stop, stop it!" I yell. I can't take it anymore. I have to get out of here! I am pushing her away from me as the overwhelming smell takes over my mind. I fly down the stairs and outside through the door Henry carved for me. I see the freshly dug dirt beside my

# janie lynn lankford
*fiction*

prized rose-bed. It suddenly hits me like a screeching siren: Henry isn't coming home at all.

I awake from a horrible dream, Rachel sitting by my side. What a dream indeed! I won't tell it to Rachel, her poor heart will break hearing the painful dream I had to suffer through the night. She talks to me timidly, like a child afraid of its own mother.

"I tried not to wake you. How are you feeling?" She asks me.

Why is she here? Have I done something unjust to her? Maybe I can start off pleasant and she will forget whatever altercation we had. She is, after all, practically my baby sister.

"Hello, Rachel!" I start. "Oh, look at the time! I need to start cleaning! Of course, I need to tidy up my hair first. Have you seen the gleam Henry gets in his eyes when he sees me with my hair nicely combed and smooth? He's the reason I work myself to the bone in this filthy house. Oh, my dear Rachel! Have you been crying? It's all right, my dear! I'm here now, and Henry will be home soon! Did you know that, Rachel? My Henry is on his way now..."

# By the Old Mill Stream

### morgan ton
*poetry*

Autumnal beauty surrounds me
The sun glows, my skin is warm
Trees slowly let their leaves go
By the Old Mill Stream.

The sky is a sea of clear blue
Flowing water whispers in my ear
It soothes my senses, my heart is full
By the Old Mill Stream.

I lie down in the sun set shadows
Drifting piles of leaves envelop me
Sunlight glistens through the fall trees
By the Old Mill Stream.

Alone, I long for the warmth of another
Anticipating their comforting words
Yearning to be wrapped in their arms
If only, it would be a perfect late fall day
By the Old Mill Stream.

# Bestest Friends

## mary catherine davidson
*fiction*

Gina had long chocolate brown hair, and I had stringy, hay-colored hair, like those stupid horses eat. She was much prettier than me, and her eyes sparkled in the light, while mine were always dull. Also, she was a whole year older than me. She was nine years old, but I was still a stupid eight-year-old baby. But no matter what, Gina was my bestest friend in the second grade.

The shiny, red minivan pulled into Gina's driveway. I jumped out of the car and ran to meet her.

"Hi Gina!" I said smiling.

"Hi! Come on, let's go upstairs." She led me upstairs to her bedroom. The walls were a soft pink color. I decided that I wanted my walls to be that color too. As I looked around, the large shelf caught my eye. It was as tall as the sky and had millions of different Barbie dolls placed neatly on each row. I'd only seen that many Barbies in the toy stores! Most of them wore long sparkly dresses and had the fun movable hair that you comb and cut. I ran over to the shelf to touch them, but Gina stopped me.

"Don't touch those, Susie! I don't wanna play Barbies, they're baby toys. Let's play rock climbers instead." She walked to the bunk beds on the opposite side of the room and began to climb the ladder.

"Come on. Follow me," I heard Gina say. I hadn't moved from the Barbies.

"Come on, Susie. Get up here!"

I looked up to where Gina was yelling at me from. It was awfully high up. I didn't want to go up. Heights were scary.

"I don't think I should," I said, turning around like I really wasn't afraid.

"Oh, come on," she said again. "You're not a scaredy cat, are you?"

I sucked in as much air as I could hold, and my lips pursed like a fishes.

"No I am not!" I stomped my foot on the ground. I hated her saying that I was a scaredy cat.

"Then come on up." She waited, but I still didn't move.

"Fine, Susie, be a baby. But I'm not friends with babies. So go away." Gina turned away so her back was facing me and humphed. I really wanted her to be my friend.

"It's not that high, you know," she said, peeking at me.

I thought about how we were gonna be best friends forever. "Ok. I...I'll come up." Gina looked pleased to get her way. I sucked in a big breath of air and held it as I walked, reluctantly, towards that ladder. I reached out for the ladder with shaking hands and grabbed hold of the cold wood. I reached for the next step. Slowly I climbed each step to the top, right hand, left hand, right foot, left foot. Seven long steps later, I made it to the top. Shaking, I clung to the princess covers on the bed. I looked around nervously, then looked down, slowly, to the ground, seeing that I wasn't too high up.

"Hey," I said, letting go of the covers a bit. "It's not too bad up here."

"Told you so." Gina replied. "Now watch this." She climbed over the safety rail onto the edge of the bunk and put her hands out in front of her. She jumped off the top bunk. A small scream came out of my mouth; I thought Gina would get hurt. However, she landed on her feet and her hands shot up into the air like the gymnasts do on TV. I looked down at her, my mouth wide open.

"Why did you do that, and leave me up here alone! How am I supposed to get down now!"

Gina giggled. "You jump, silly. That's the whole fun of getting up there."

"No way! I won't jump and you can't make me. Let's just play Barbies." I turned around and inched my way to the ladder, but before I got there Gina had gotten there first and unhooked the ladder. There wasn't any way down now.

"This isn't funny Gina!" I sobbed. "Let me down." She didn't move. She would get her way, again. I inched my way forward to the railing and carefully slipped my feet over the railing. First my right foot, then my left foot. With tingly arms, I put my hands out in front of me like Gina did.

I couldn't back down now; I was close to jumping. I wasn't sure if Gina would put the ladder back if I didn't jump. But, if I didn't jump, and she did put the ladder back, I would be a scaredy cat and a baby forever. Then I wouldn't have a bestest friend anymore. I had to jump.

I sucked in my last breath of air and held it, my cheeks puffing out. I looked to the ground, but it was much farther away than before. I knew I was scared, but I would never, ever admit that to Gina. I leaned a

# mary catherine davidson
*fiction*

little more off the railing.  Finally, I jumped off the railing, and all of the air I had sucked in flew out of my mouth in a scream.

I hit the ground.  It felt like I landed on a gazillion nails.  I started crying, my whole body hurting.  I heard faint footsteps in the hallway, but I felt someone touch my arm and heard them gasp.  I knew it was Gina's dad.  His warm hands lifted me and carried me away.  I knew I was in the car when I heard the engine roar.

An eternity later, I opened my eyes.  I was in a white room with jungle animals on the walls.  A lady with a red cross on her hat was reaching over me.  When she saw me awake, she smiled and said that she would go get my dad.  But it wasn't my dad who entered the room, it was Gina and her daddy.  He knelt down by my side and talked quietly.

"Honey, you don't have any broken bones, just some bruises.  You're going to be all right.  Ok?"  I nodded my head and started to cry.

"I think Gina wants to talk to you.  I'll be in the hallway if you need me."  He left the room and Gina took the place where her dad was just standing.

"Hi, Susie," Gina said, looking at her shoes, and twisting back and forth.

"Susie, will you forgive me?"  But I didn't want to forgive her.  She called me a baby, then made me jump from the bunk bed.  I never wanted to be friends with her again.

"Please, Susie," she begged, "I'm really sorry I called you a baby and made you jump off the bunk bed.  I really wanna be your friend again."

I stared into her sparkly eyes, unmoving.  She did look very sorry, and I did want to be her friend too, deep inside.  I smiled at her and nodded.  A large smile appeared on her face, and her eyes got glossy, like she was going to cry.  We really were going to be bestest friends forever.

"You know, Susie, I think you have very sparkly eyes."

# Nest of Needles

**minyoung choi**
*sketch*

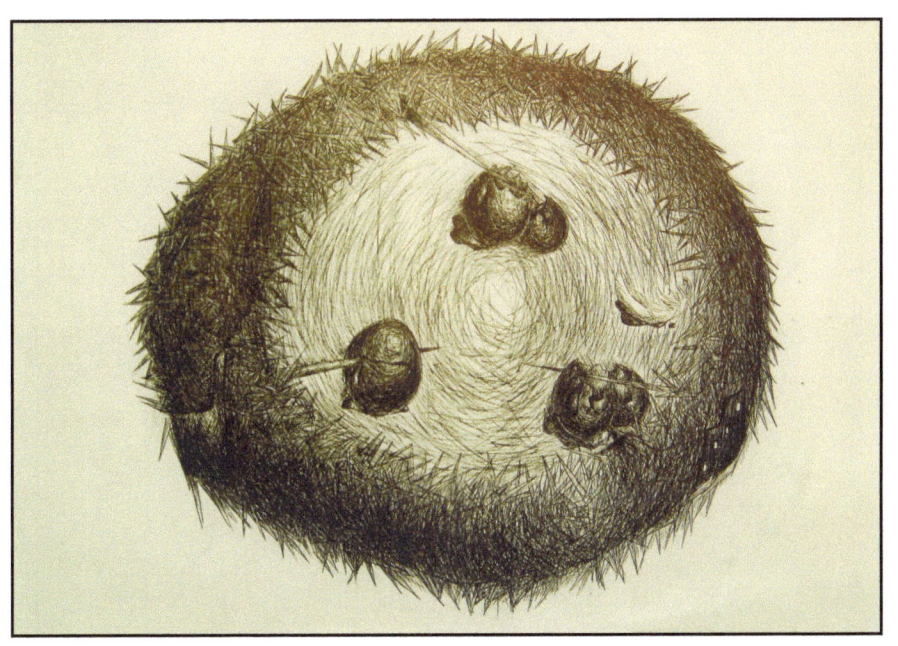

# Where Do We Go From Here?

**katie mcmurray**
*photograph*

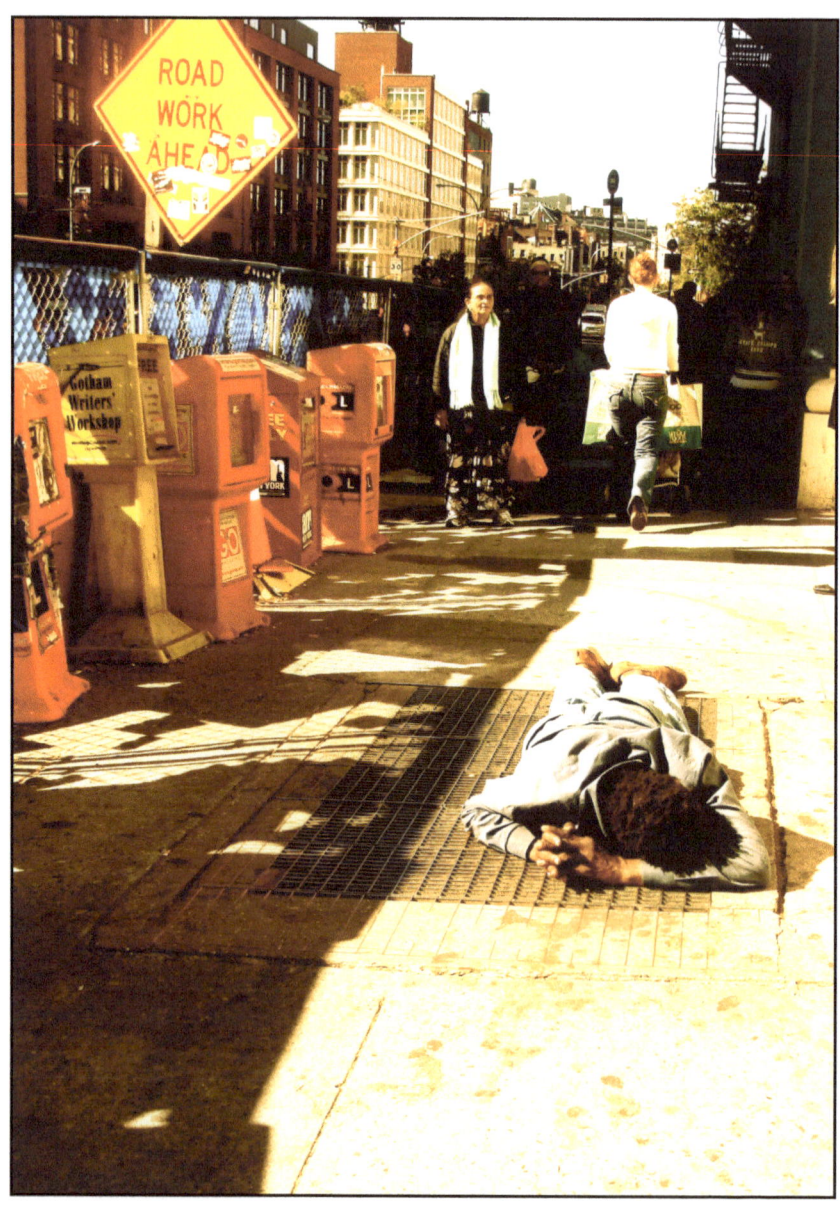

# My Savior

## amy hein
### *fiction*

As I am standing on the edge of a cliff, I watch the beautiful sea as it sparkles in the sunlight. There is a slight breeze that is hitting my face. Dolphins are swimming and playing below. Birds are flying and singing above. Everything is so peaceful and so at ease.

Off in the distance, the sky is growing dark. The gentle breeze that was caressing my face just moments ago is now a strong gale. The whole sky is now black. Out of stubborn pride I refuse to leave as I stand there amazed by the beautiful lightning as it dances across the sky. My instinct is telling me to go but my mind says just stay awhile longer...

The next thing that I know there is a loud crack and the ground begins to tremble. There is another large gust of wind, which pushes me over the edge of the cliff. I am falling! Falling so fast that I can hardly grasp the concept of what is happening. After what seemed to be forever, I hit the restless water. Waves are crashing from every direction. I struggle to stay at the surface. My arms and legs are burning as they begin to grow tired. I keep trying. The sea with all of his wrath and strength forces me into his grasp. At this moment, I realize that there is nothing more that I can do. My lungs are burning for air as I struggle to keep my breath in and the water out.

Just as I begin to give up, a large, strong hand finds mine. A kind, confident voice is telling me to take it. The second that I take hold of it, I am out of the water and safe on land. The kind voice belongs to a man with a pleasant face and a warm smile. He wraps me up in a warm blanket and takes me in His arms. He is lovingly stroking my hair as He says, "I love you my child. You are safe now, I am here. I always have been and I always will be."

As I look around me, I realize that the sun is shining again: the storm is now over. I glance at His face with both amazement and bewilderment. Then I look at His hands and feet. Here I see the scars. I look back up to see Him smiling at my stunned expression. He nods His head and simply says, "I am."

# Chicago in the Snow

**erin channell**
*photograph*

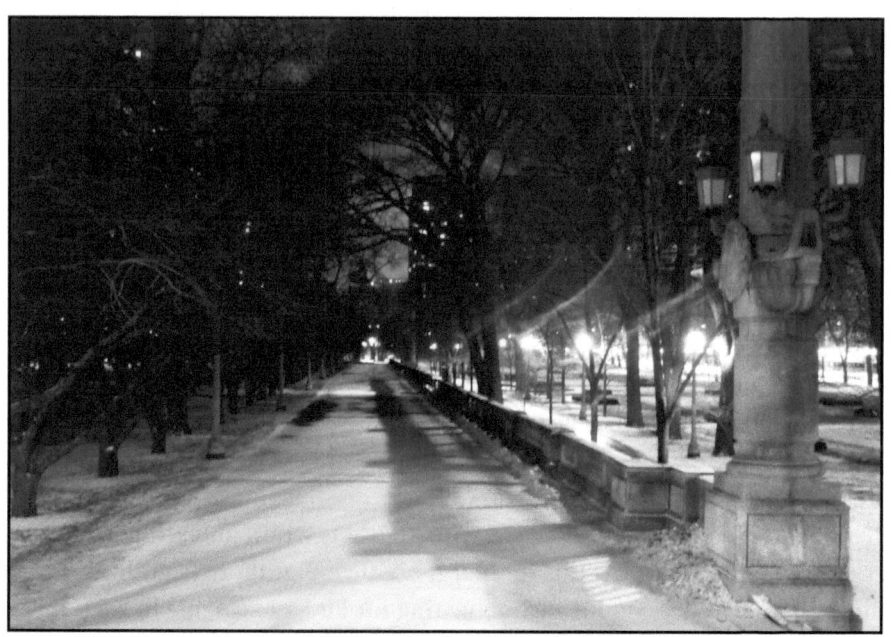

# Dusk

### erin channell
*photograph*

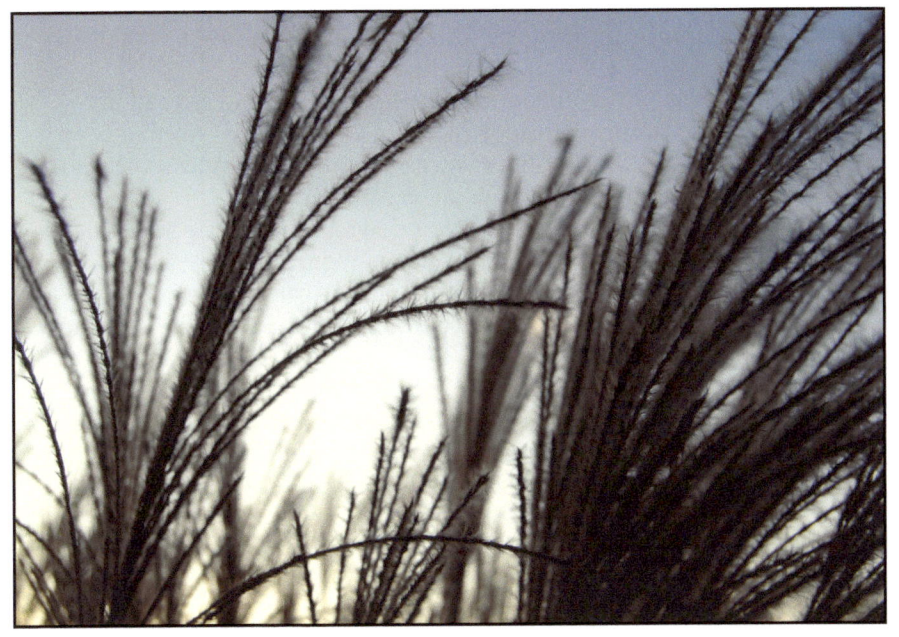

# Truth is Stranger Than Fiction

## dona howell
*fiction*

She looks familiar to me.  She looks like someone I have known before – someone from my past.  But different, somehow.  Her eyes are a little vacant.  She is anxious, troubled, a little frantic.  She keeps looking around, wringing her hands, pacing back and forth – searching for something.

"Where's Nancy?"

I just look at her – my own eyes now blank.  "Who?"

"Nancy!  I can't find her.  Do you know where she is?"

My mind is now blank.  Who is this lady?  Who is she looking for?  Why is she so upset?

As I look around, I tell her that I don't know where Nancy is.  "Maybe she's outside."

The woman glances out the door and, almost immediately, repeats her behavior.

"Where's Nancy?"

Now I'm not sure that I have seen this woman before.  Here is a grown woman, frantically hunting for something that she's not really trying to find.

I'm getting a little uncomfortable here.  I pretend to read my magazine.  All the time my mind is racing.  Why does this woman keep asking me these questions?  I hear voices outside – why doesn't she go out there and see if one of those people is Nancy?

Thank goodness the sun is going down.  I'll go home soon, and then I won't have to deal with this strange person.

I try to concentrate on my magazine.

"Are you sure that you haven't seen Nancy?  I can't find her anywhere!"

This is so simple.  Nancy's definitely not inside.  This woman has searched every corner of the house for her.  Over and over.  All the lady has to do is step outside and see if Nancy is out there.  How hard can this be?  I know that it is getting darker outside – but there is still enough light left for her to be able to find the girl that she is looking for.

"I think that Nancy's outside.  Why don't you check out there?"

Once again she gets as far as the door and then turns back.  Her brown eyes are anxious.  She twists her long brown fingers together.  Her voice is rising as she repeats her request.

"I can't find Nancy anywhere."

Suddenly I see past the confusion, and the reality of what is happening sends a chill through me.  The woman, who is old enough to be a grandmother, is looking for her lost child.  At least, a child that she thinks she has lost.

I will always remember this day.  As this woman's brain becomes more clouded by Alzheimer's, my mind suddenly becomes clearer as to what the future holds for her, for me, and for her lost child.

I can't change the future – or the past.  But I can comfort her and help her today as she begins to slip from my reality into hers.

Putting down the magazine, I take her hand.

"Come on, Mother.  I'll help you find my sister."

*In loving memory of my mother Marjorie Harrell Lowry*
*September 6, 1920-July 3, 2003*

# Haiku

## matthew anderson
*poetry*

### FISH

Ride the sea's currents
Scales like the tropical sun
No cares in the world

### JUNGLE CAT

Orange and black cat
A deep growl is emitted
It is feeding time

### MATCH

Strike on the rough side
Intense release of bright light
Smoke fills up the air

# Water Words and Reflections

### sarah heath
*photograph*

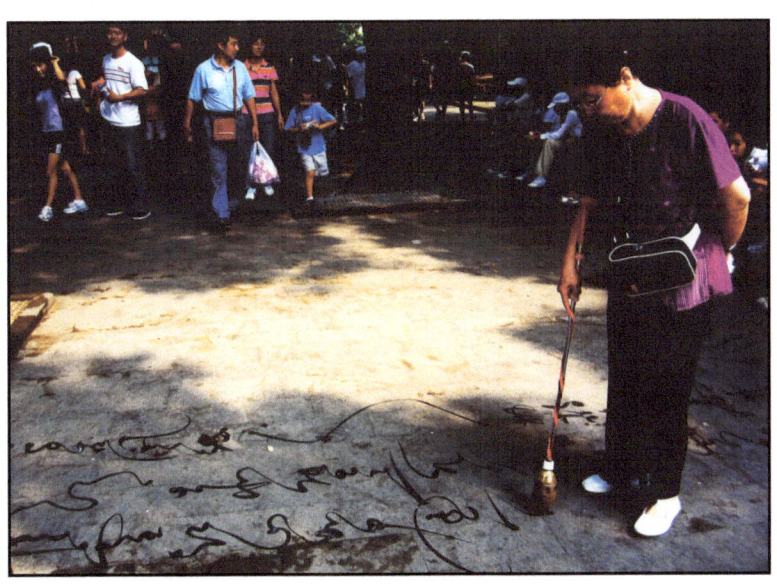

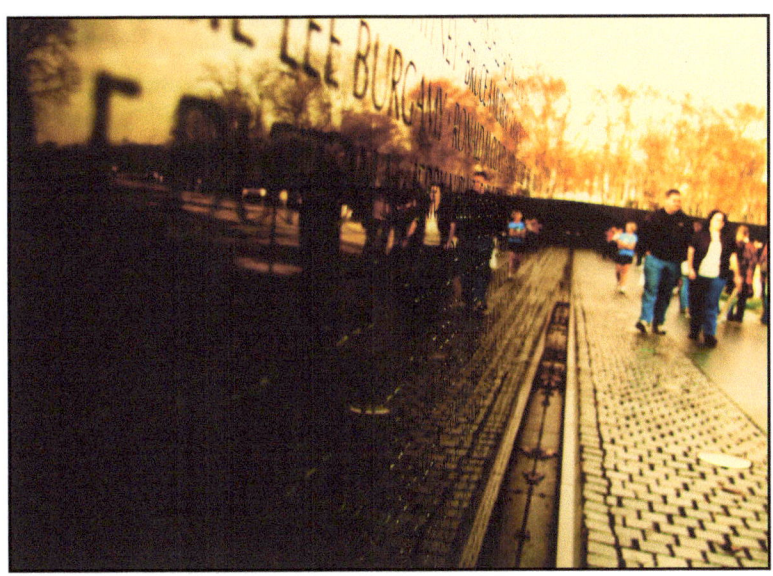

# Break Through the Night

## haley criswell
*silhouette*

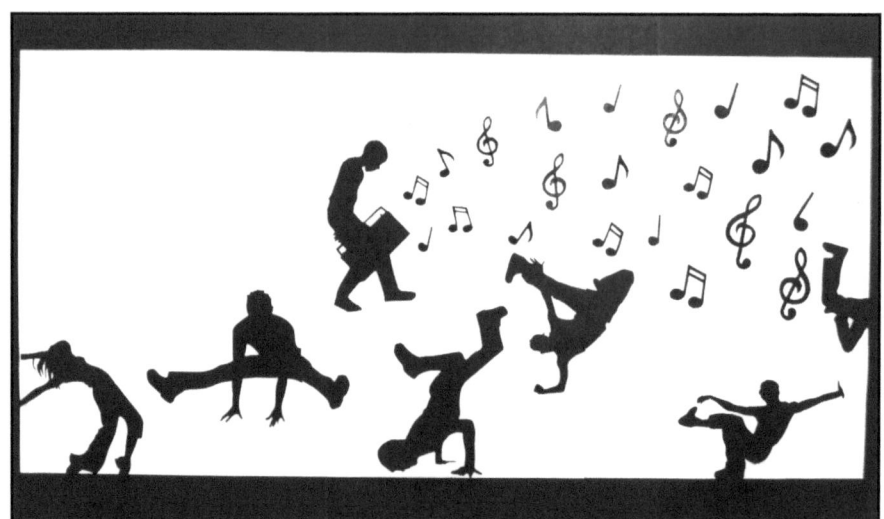

# Summer's Fire

**dolci sanders**
*photograph*

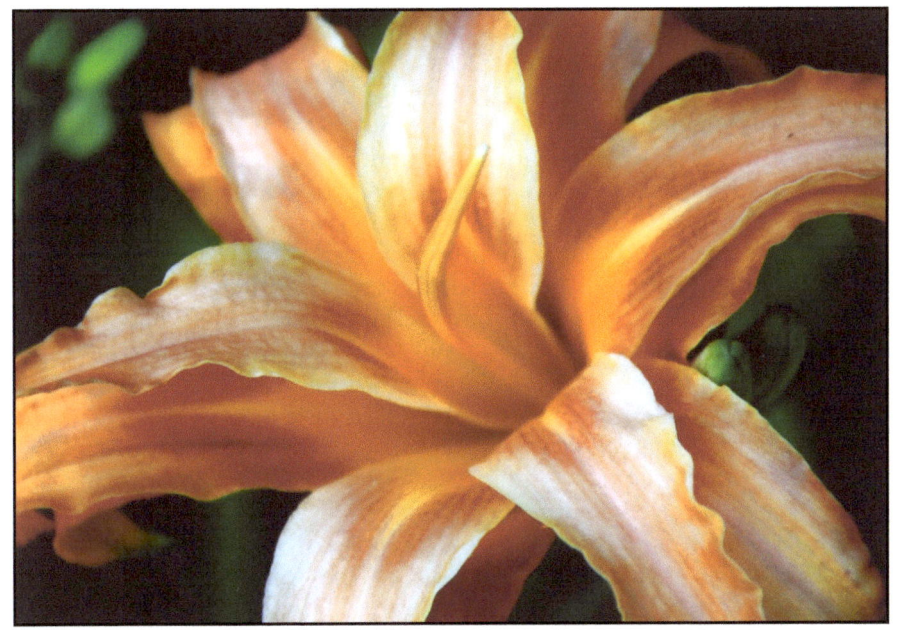

# The Most Deadly Valentine

## allison loftis
### creative nonfiction

On January 8th, 1929, I picked up the body of my best friend, Pasquillano Lolordo, off of the bloody streets of Chicago. Half of his face was blown off, and there were perfectly round holes in his chest that were the size of a man's fist. On this day I, Alphonse Capone, vow to execute George Moran, the murderer of my friend. On February 14th, 1929, Valentine's Day, Mr. Moran will receive the most deadly valentine.

It is the day before Valentine's Day and everything is going to be exactly as planned. I arranged a message to be sent from a man in Detroit to Mr. Moran two days ago saying that a special gift of three truck-loads of hijacked whiskey was to be delivered to his garage on 2121 North Clark Street. Mr. Moran received the message this morning. He will be waiting outside of his garage for the trucks. Five of my men and I will drive up in a police car, dressed in uniform. I will first kill Mr. Moran. Then I will leave after I know Mr. Moran has half his face blown off and holes in his chest the size of two men's fists. I will leave any other men that were with Mr. Moran to be silenced by my men. It will be the bloodiest Valentine in history.

February 14th has finally come. It is the day of my revenge. So far everything is going as planned. I got into my police uniform. It has the smell of death on it. The smell I have been longing for. It is 7 o'clock in the morning and the city of Chicago seemed to be still and quiet. It seemed peaceful. It was the perfect day for a murder. One of my men brought in six machine guns, loaded and ready to assassinate. When I took one of the guns I felt like I had all of the power in this world. I felt angry and vengeful toward Mr. Moran. He will pay with his blood. The police car came to our warehouse. All six of us got into the car. As we got closer, it started to rain. It was raining so hard I couldn't see outside of my window. I started to worry. I thought that he wasn't going to be there because of the rain. The driver told me that we were at the garage. I rolled down my window and I saw three men outside of the garage. None of the three men were George Moran.

I was bothered. I was annoyed. I was furious. When we ran out of the car, we were yelling at the men to open the garage. There were four other men in the garage. None of them were Mr. Moran. I yelled at them to put their hands in the air and to face the wall. There was a dog tied up to a bumper of a car. It was barking and howling piercingly. I spat in its face, and then I silenced it with three shots. I started to search the place for Mr. Moran. He wasn't here. I asked one of the men to tell me where he was. "I will tell you nothing, you disgusting street rat," he said. This made me very angry. So I shot him in the head seven times. I went to another man and asked him the same question. "He is in a meeting," the man said nervously. "Thank you," I replied. "Can you tell me where he is?" I said. "I don't know," the man said. I put the gun in his mouth. I could feel his breathing quickening. I smiled. His eyes filled with fear. Then I shot him. His blood splattered on my sleeve. As I looked down at the dead man, he had the same look on his face as my friend did. His eyes were wide open with fear, and blood was oozing out of his ears. I looked up with an unsympathetic expression on my face. "Do any of you know where George Moran's meeting is being held?" I asked. They all shook their heads no. I was disappointed. "Kill them all," I commanded my men with an evil grin.

As I started to walk out of the garage, it stopped raining. I could hear the gun shots. I could hear the screams of terror from the fearful men. They were all dead by the time I exited the garage. Blood was everywhere, and it seemed to paint a picture of mortality. The smell of death did not satisfy me. The terror in the men's eyes did not satisfy me. As I stepped into the car, anger and frustration fell upon me. Before I got in, I looked back at the garage. Staring at the building, I yelled at the top of my lungs, "George Moran, the next day you see my face will be the day you die!"

*Based on the True Story of the Saint Valentine Massacre*

# Pinkerton Park

**matt gordon**
*photograph*

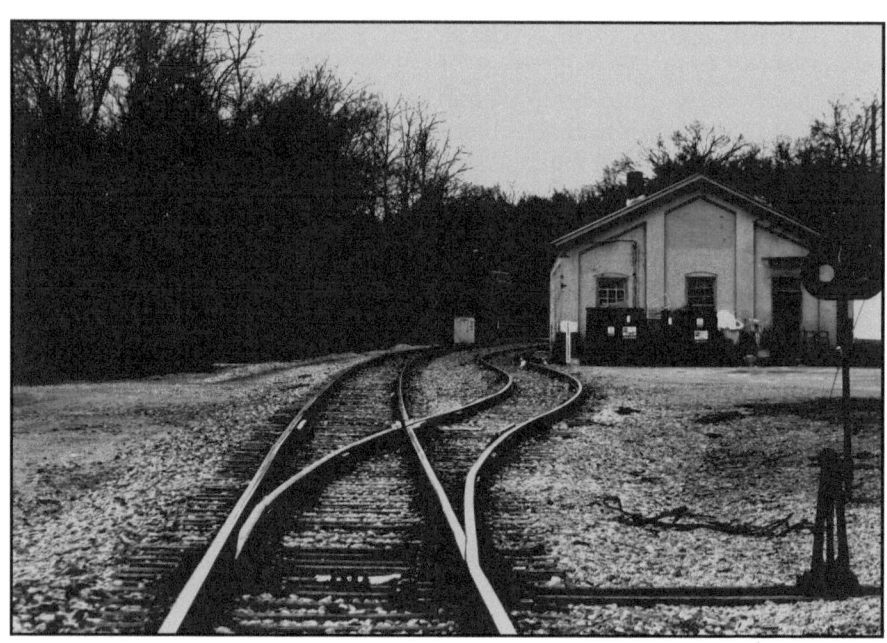

# Drink of Water

**matt gordon**
*photograph*

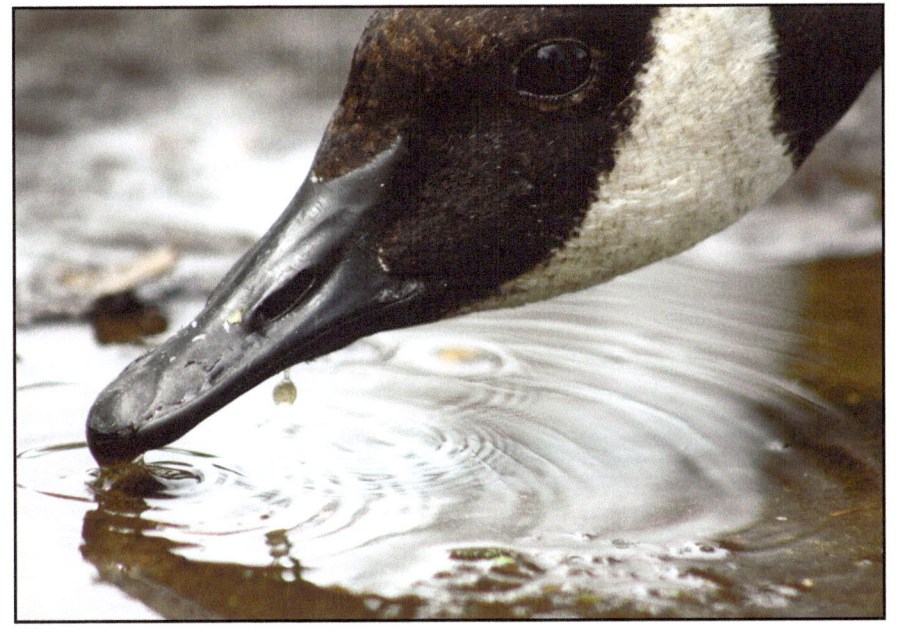

# Rage

## katie gass
*creative nonfiction*

Storming through the back door, the enraged man enters. The crowded room jumps from their seats to see the problem at hand. Yelling ensues, and the fighting begins. After being repeatedly told not to show up at the family gathering, the monster insists and makes his appearance. I soon realize that our traditional family gathering is about to take a turn for the worse. As the only one not presently engaged in the argument, I bolt to the quiet safety of the car. What I thought was a refuge, soon turns out to be a front row view of the altercation ahead.

Staring in astonishment from the backseat window, I witness my uncle shove my mother. After this physical act of violence, the shrieking and shouting continue to escalate. I sit in shock watching this fight take place on what was supposed to be a peaceful afternoon. Some forceful coaxing from my father forces my uncle to leave the driveway, never to return. About thirty minutes later, to our complete surprise, someone knocks on the door. Thinking that this demon-like man has returned, we look up only to find two burly police officers making their way into the kitchen. Shaking like a scared animal from the nervousness over the situation, I answer the questions from the officers. Monotonous question after question reveal that all sitting in the living room are innocent in the matter, and that it is my uncle that must be dealt with legally.

Sitting in the back of a police cruiser is something I thought I would never see my mother do. Although completely innocent in the situation, strict protocol says she must be transported by an officer to obtain a restraining order against my uncle. Sliding out of the backseat and putting her feet to the pavement, my mother is back with us again, with order in hand. I am relieved the situation is resolved. Noses turning cold from the winter air, my family and I ponder the day. I can only hope that Christmas Day will be much less eventful than the Christmas Eve I just experienced.

# The Experience of Exhaustion

## peng (dana) zhang
### *creative nonfiction*

Three, two, one…" Ring… The lagging bell finally signaled the end of this long-lasting Friday! I stood up from my chair, clumsily lifted up my over-loaded backpack, and reluctantly put it on my weary shoulders. Joining the crowd languidly, I went into the garage and found my bike standing stiffly among the compacted bicycles. With a helpless sigh, I stepped forward to untangle the twisted bike handles and separated my bike from the others. Getting out of the garage, I expected to breathe in some fresh air after a day's indoor life, but what welcomed me was the intense sunlight that suddenly glared at my face and blinded my eyes. Although it was an afternoon in September, the piercing sun had not waned. On the street, I pedaled slowly and looked about the surroundings to distract my focus on the exhaustion I felt. The trees and grass remained silent and still as the commanding wind lost its track. A few dogs with droopy eyes lay under the trees instead of rapidly lolling their tongues and barking at the bikers and walkers. The routinely hasty cars, as well, were too drowsy to scream at the slow bikers, who crossed cautiously in front of them. The entire city seemed slumberous.

As I continued on my way home, I felt the sweat trickling on my face and my back. Eight miles, at that time to me, was an endless trip. What was worse, my mischievous backpack was putting more and more pressure on my shoulders. The pedals on my bike became harder and harder to depress. A red traffic light surprisingly became my rescue this time. I stopped at a red light and waited unusually patiently for the light to turn green. After this short five-minute break, my weariness apparently lessened as the frantic beating of my heart gradually dropped into a slower rhythm. My bike, at the same time, showed relief through its reduced resistance. Ten minutes later, I reached our beautiful apartment building with great consolation. After parking my laborious bike in the garage, I staggered to my parents' apartment on the third floor breathless. Pleased by the well air-conditioned room, I gave a big smile to my amiable parents and sank into the softest couch in the living room…

# Umbrellas

**katie mcmurray**
*photograph*

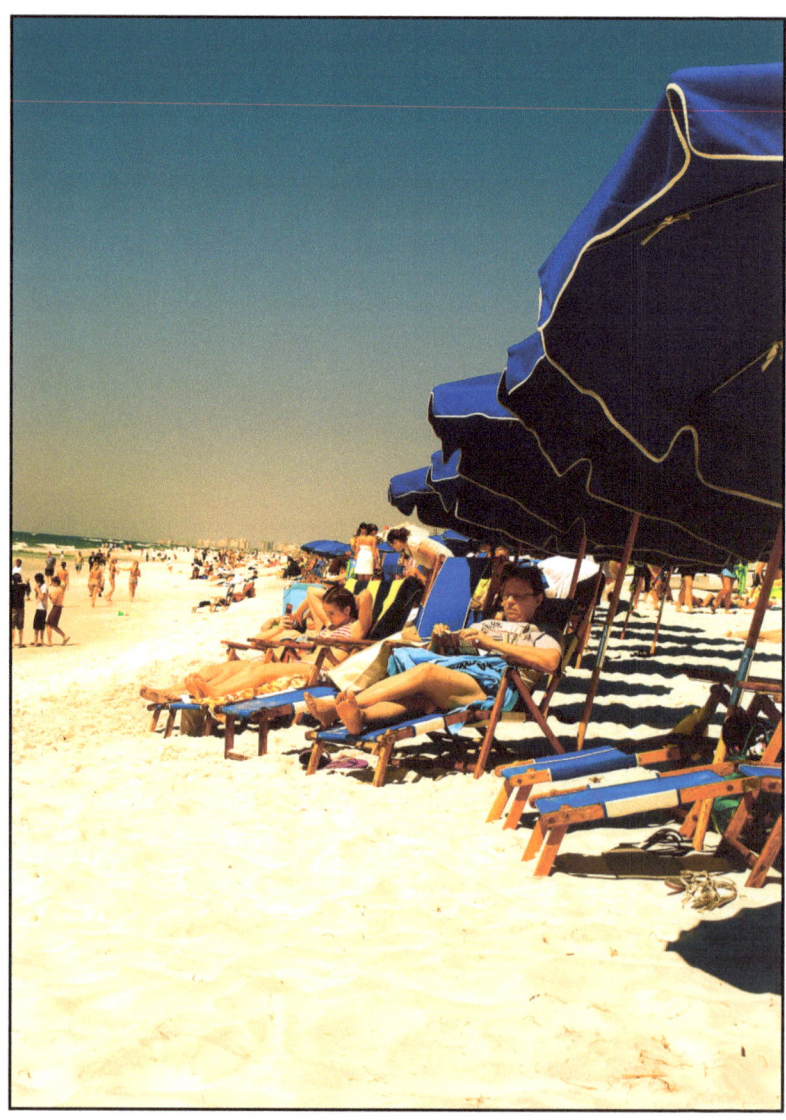

# The Odyssey Poem

## reid finchem
*poem*

Long, long ago
Odysseus and his crew
Set off and sailed the ocean blue
So Homer and his scholar friends,
Could bring this epic poem to you,

They left to fight the Trojan War,
That seems like quite a daunting chore,
Upon their famous trip back home
On and on it seemed to drone.
Among the adventures they beheld,
Avoiding the trance of the Siren's spell,

Imprisonment by a beast with just one eye,
Who spoke a Prayer of their demise;
Temptation of the lotus fruits
Overcome the many of sailing brutes.
After eating Apollo's scared colts,
Zeus struck them with a thunderbolt.

His men reduced only to bones
Odysseus now travels all alone,
He tells his story to a Phaeacian King,
And to his home he'll gladly bring
On arrival in Ithaca,
Odysseus receives help from Athena,

And right before his very eyes, she
Gives to him a beggar's guise,
He goes back to his former palace
And kills the suitors with much malice
He shot an arrow through twelve axe heads
And now he sleeps in his own bed.

# Holly y Alfredo

## moriah farmer
*photograph*

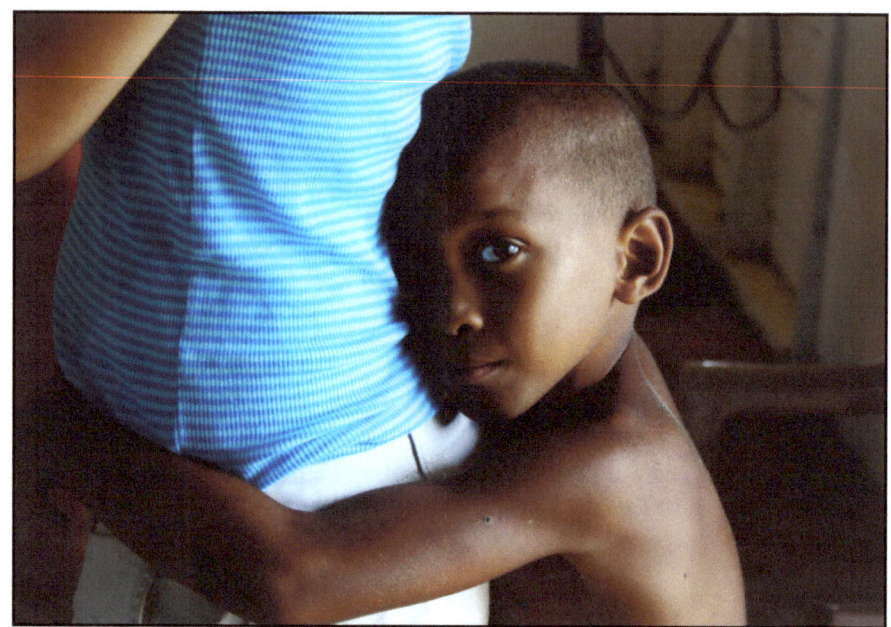

# Slavery Stitched

**elizabeth bacon**
*sketch*

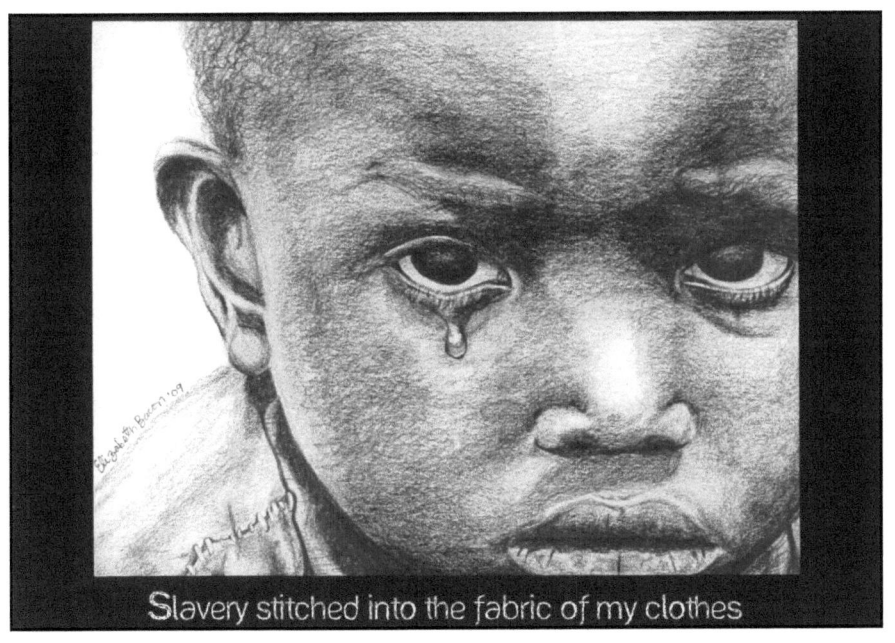

Slavery stitched into the fabric of my clothes